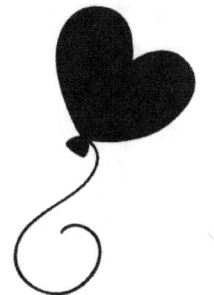

This

Cute Animals & Fruits, Toddler

Coloring Book.

belongs to

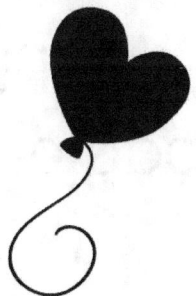

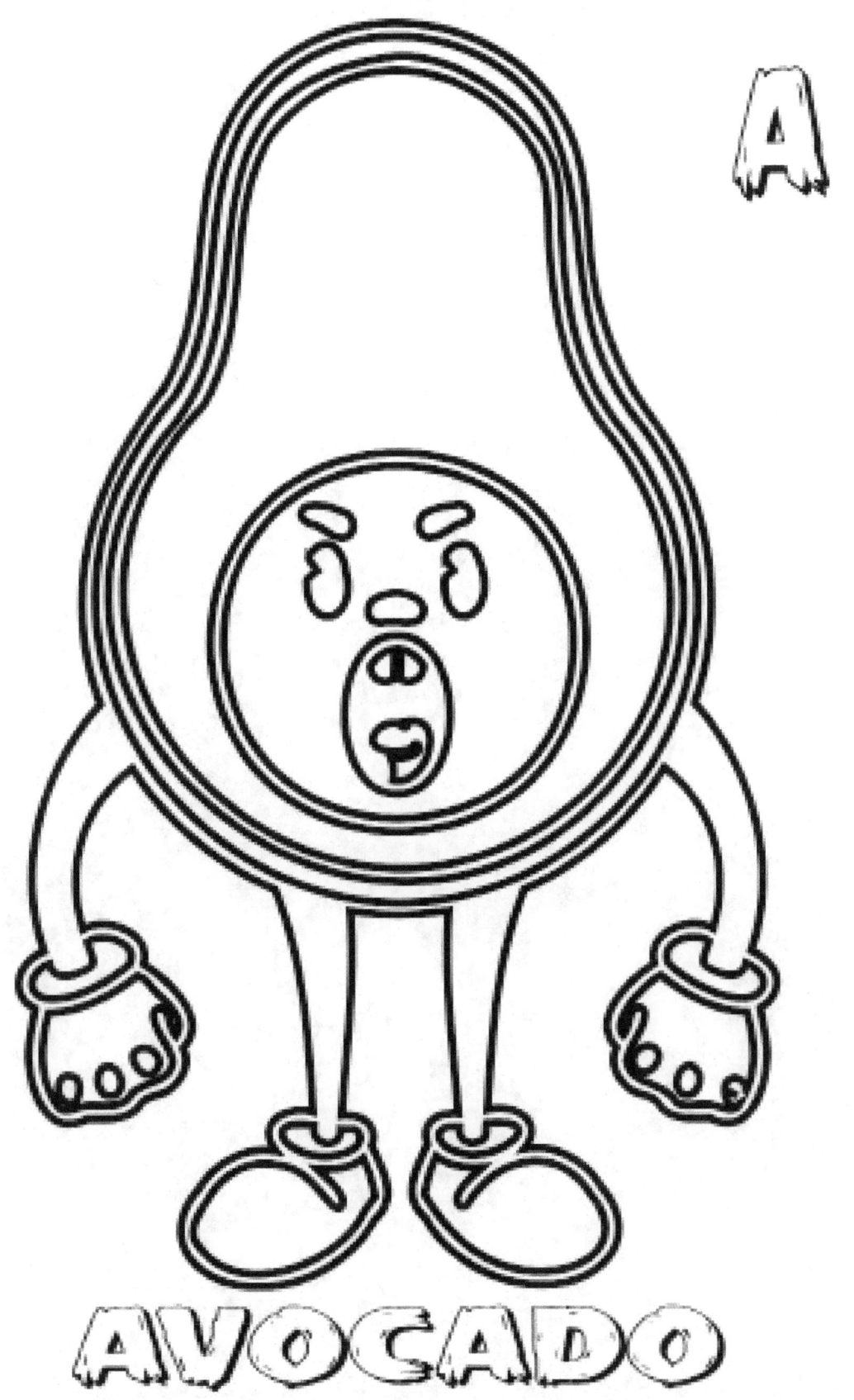

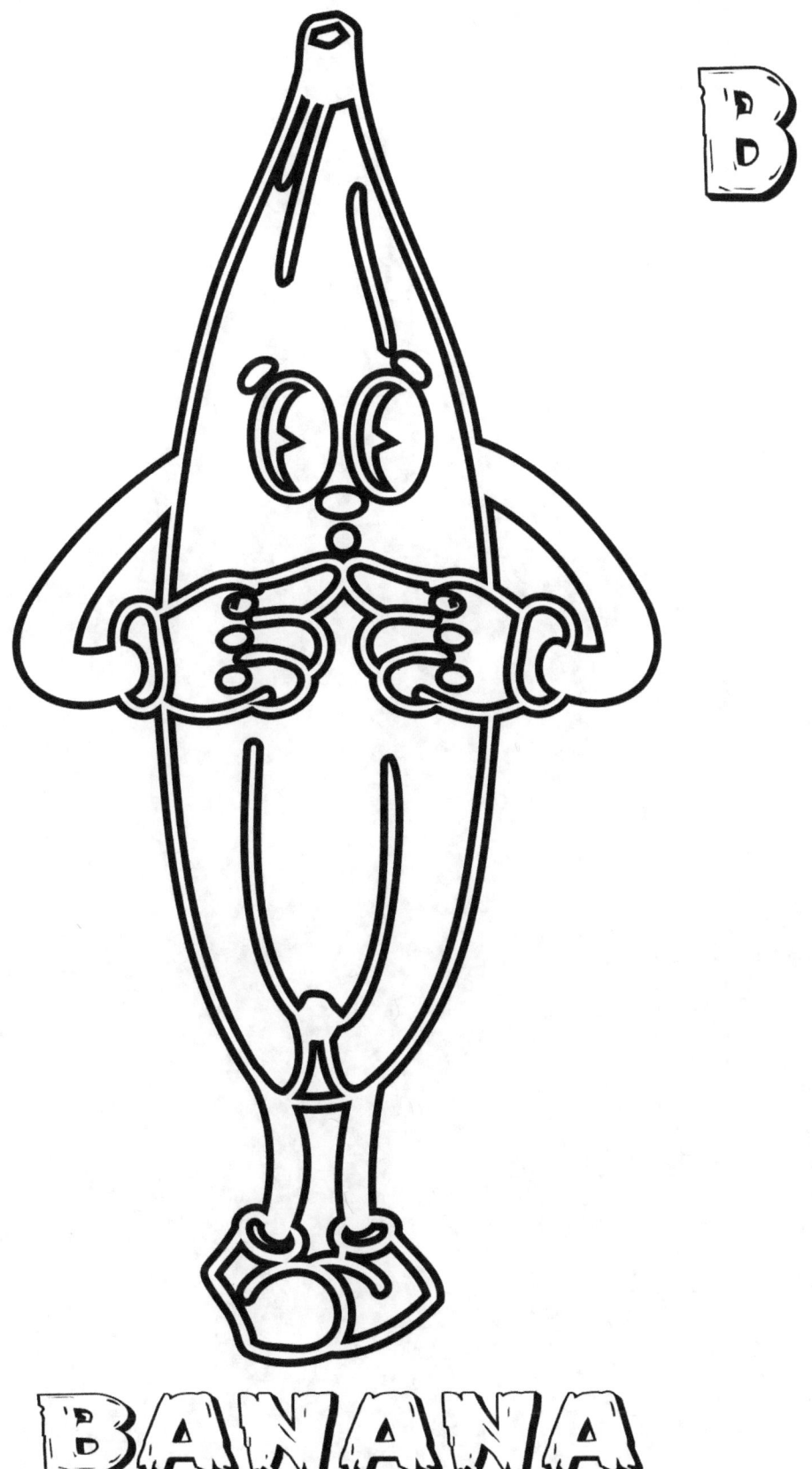

BANANA

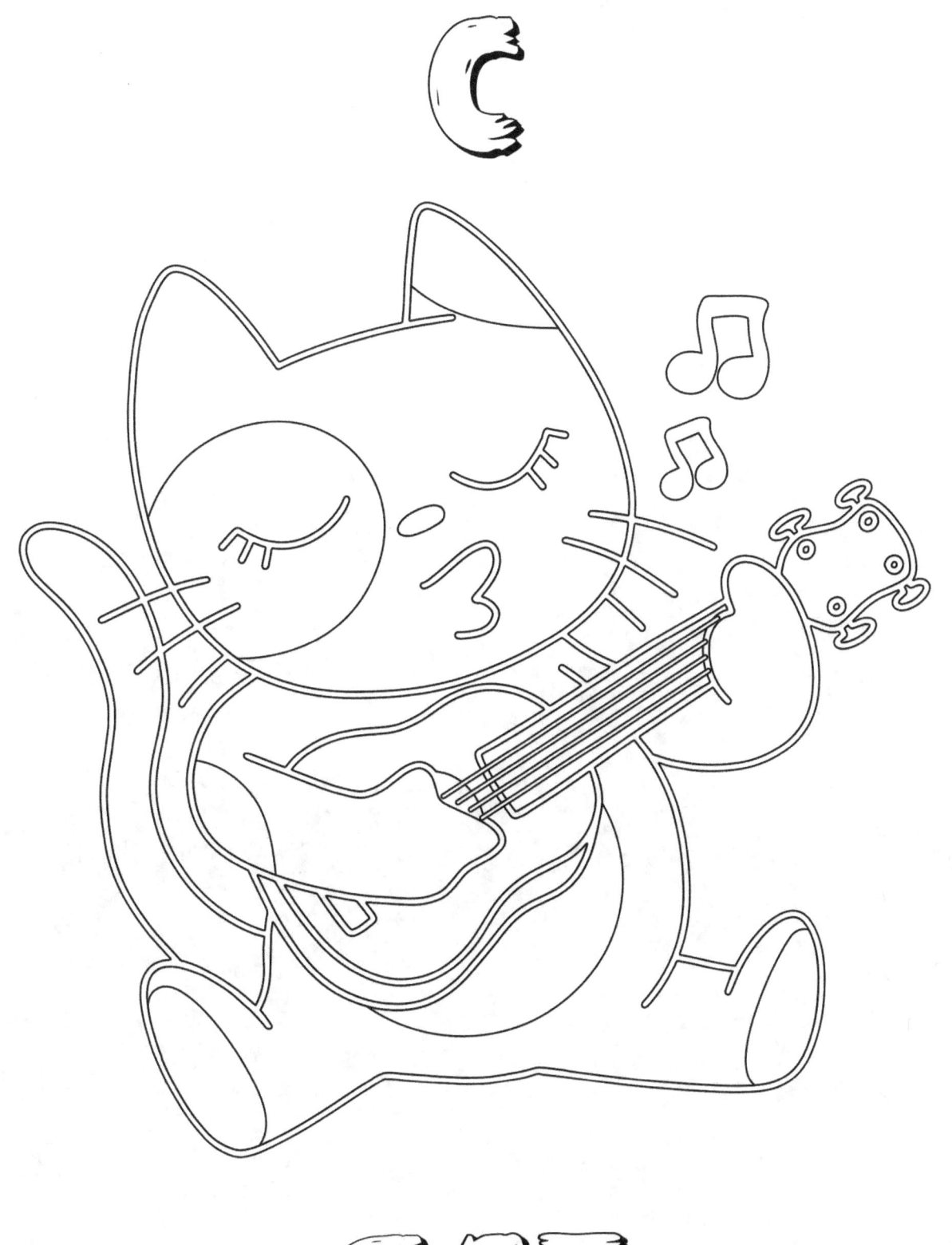

D

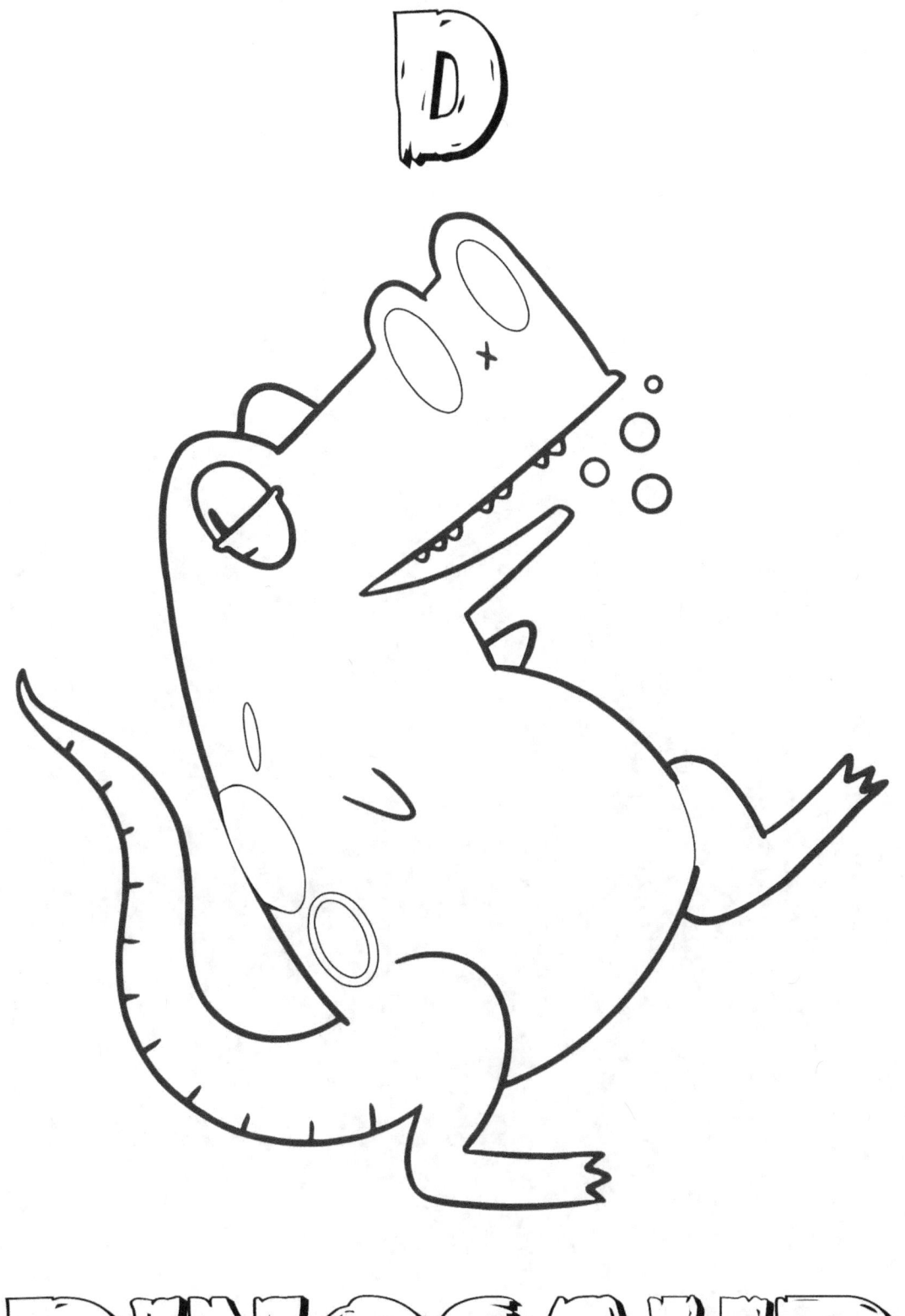

DINOSAUR

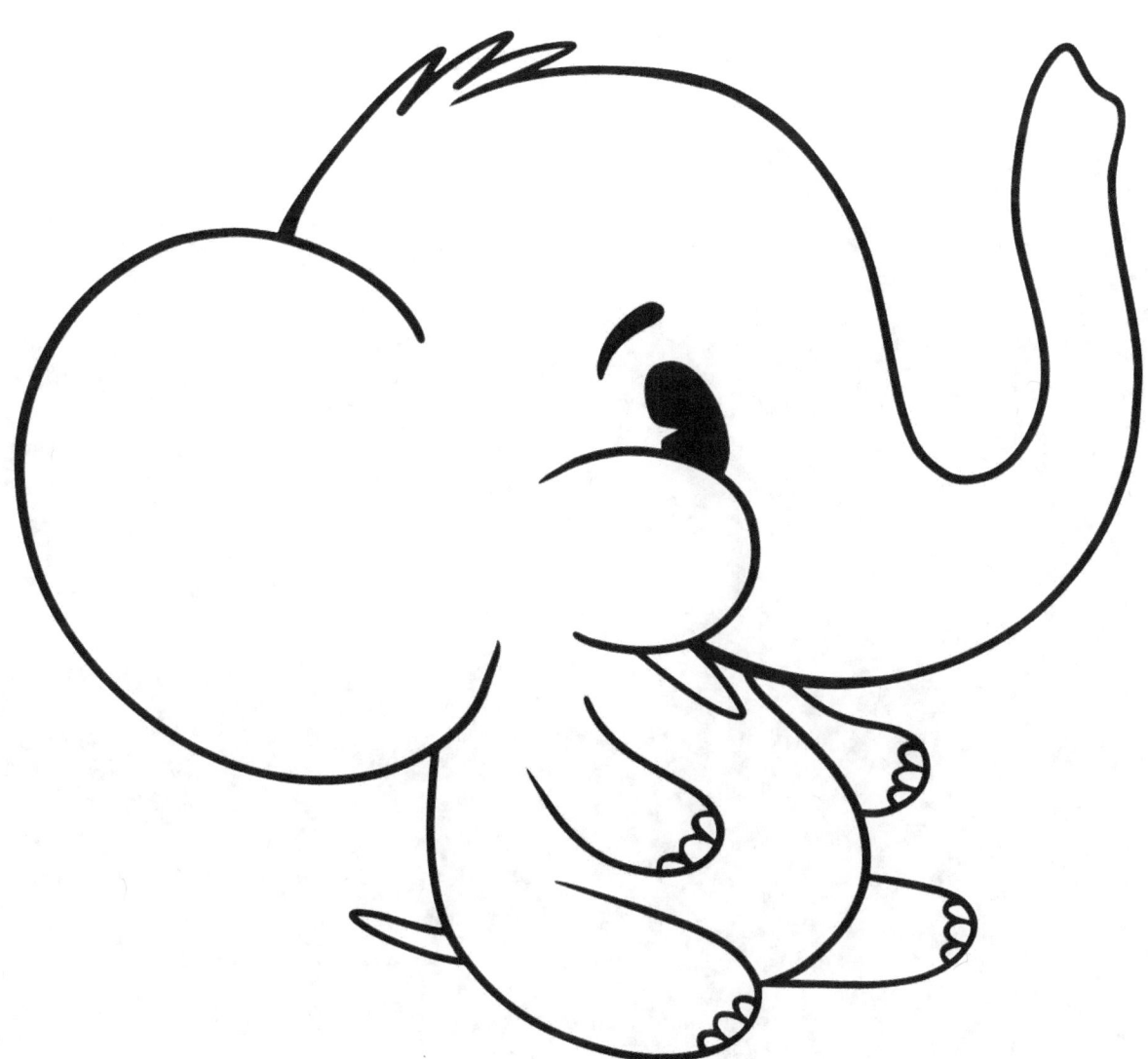

ELEPHANT

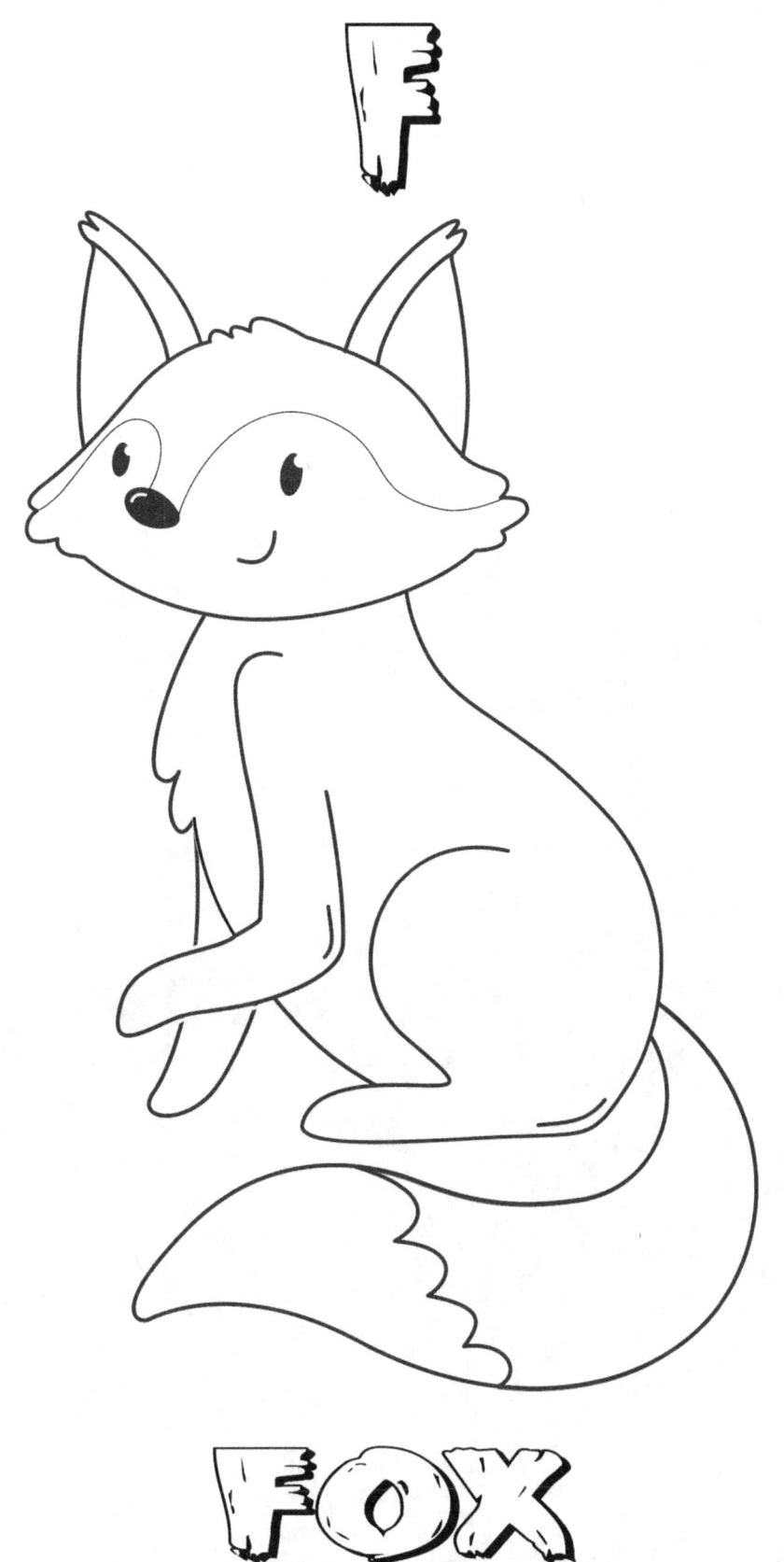

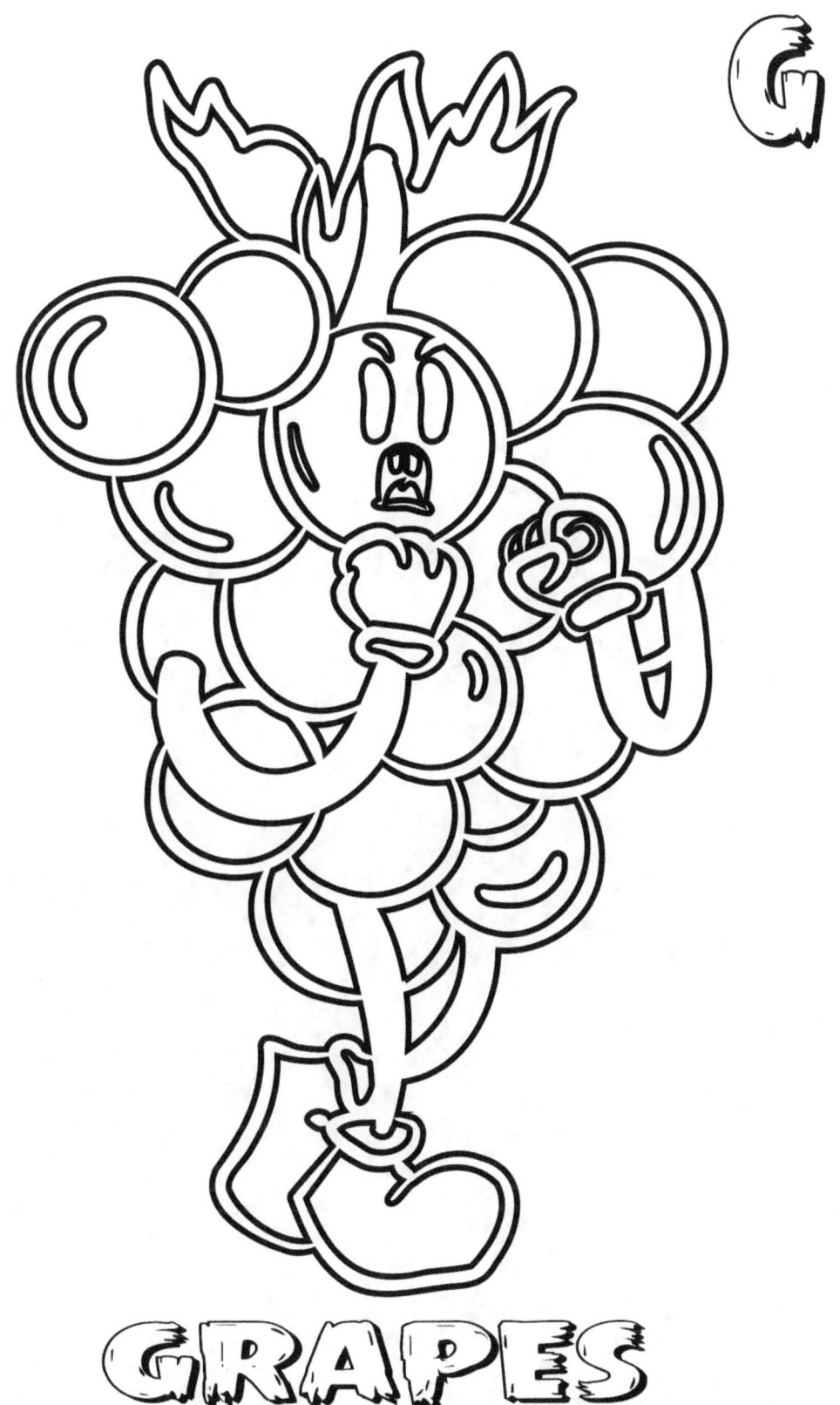

GRAPES

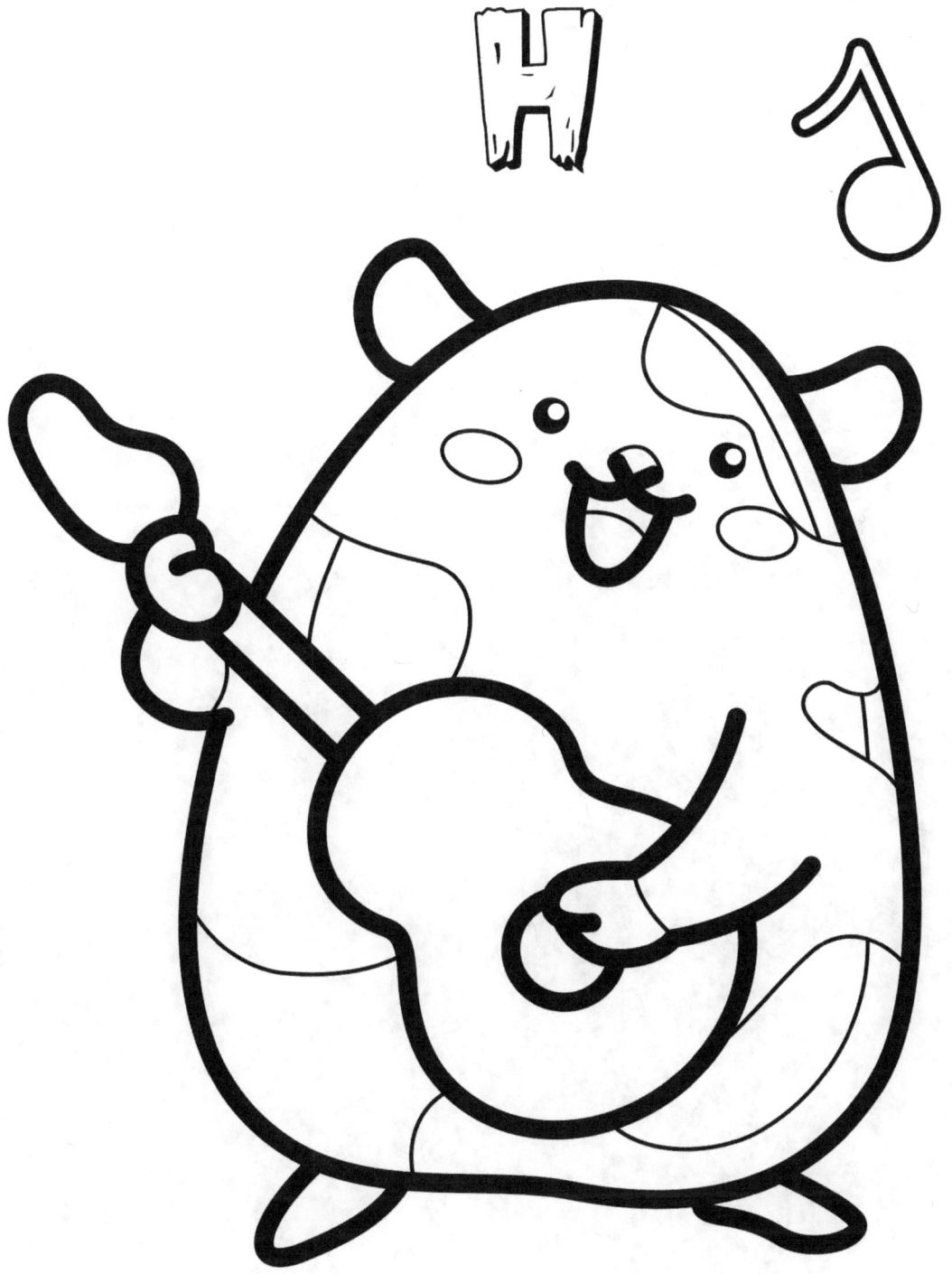

H

HAMSTER

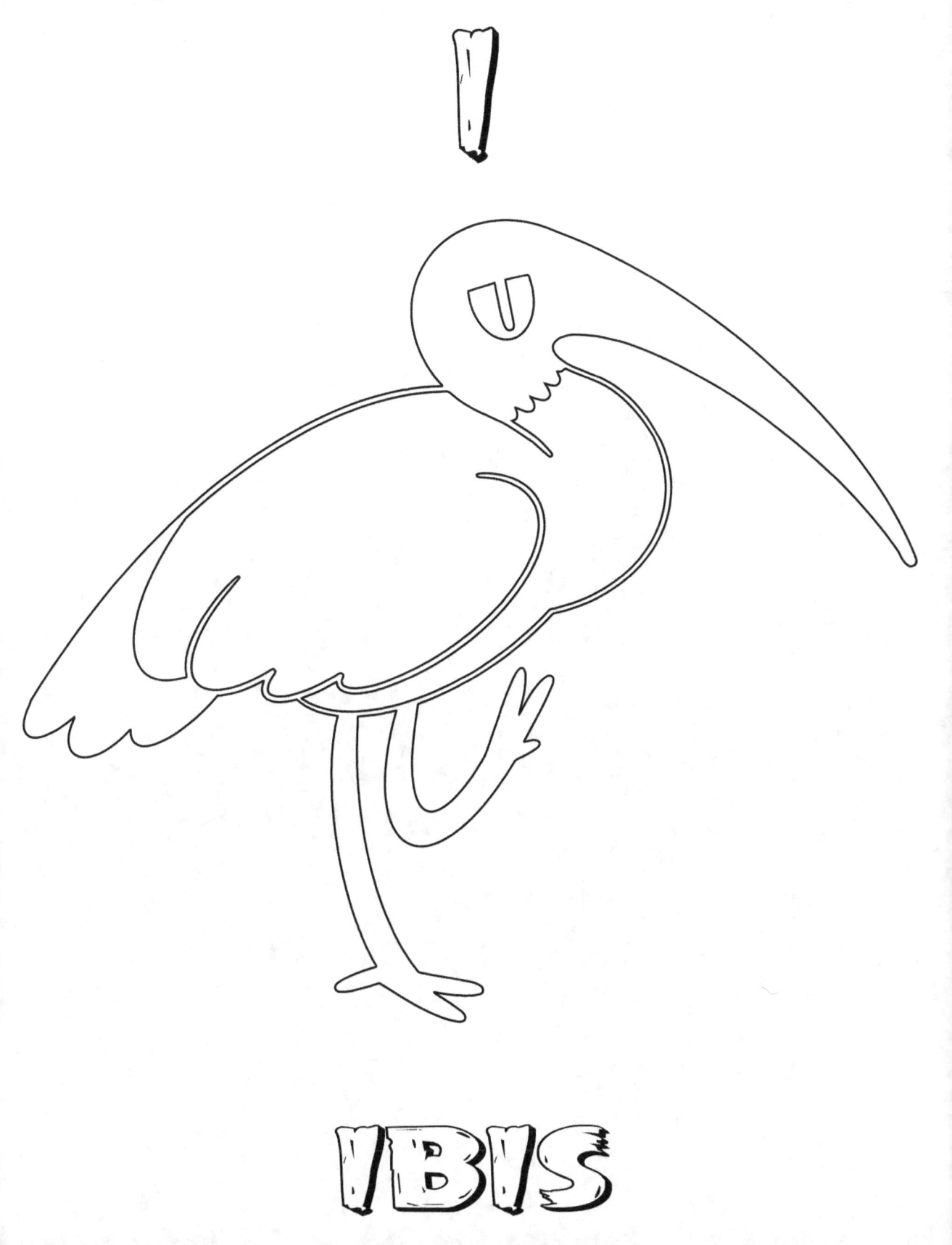

IBIS

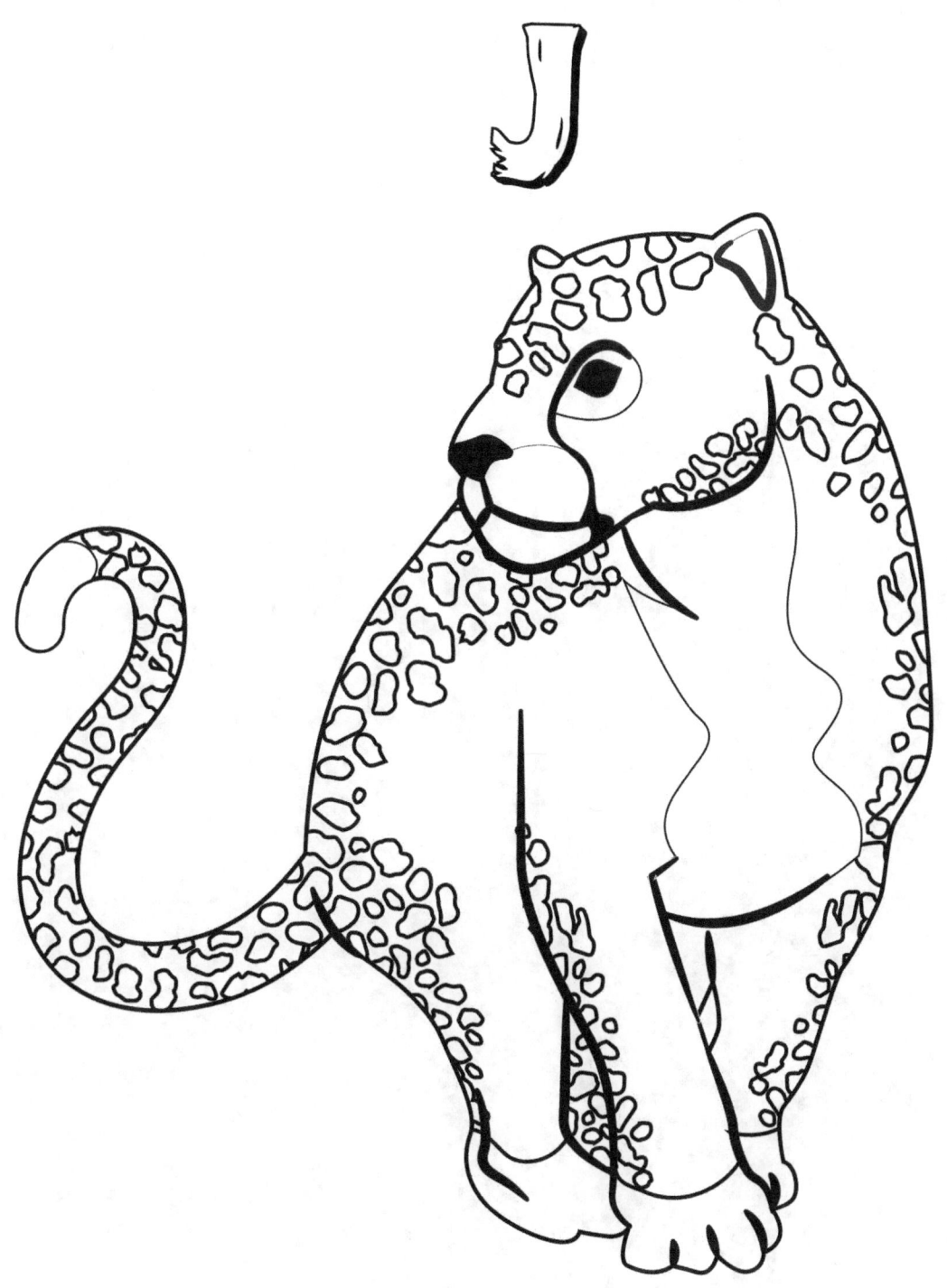

J

JAGUAR

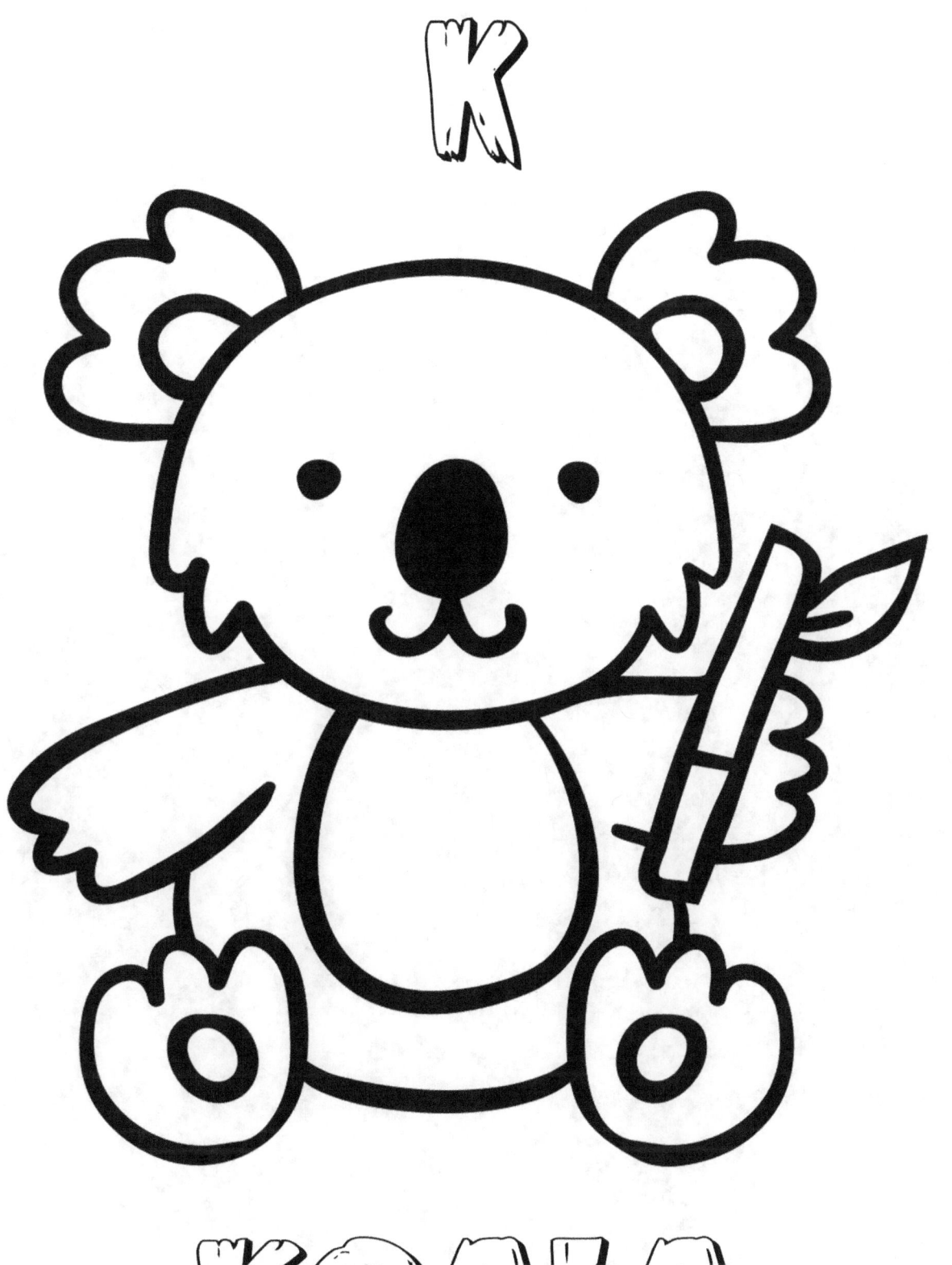

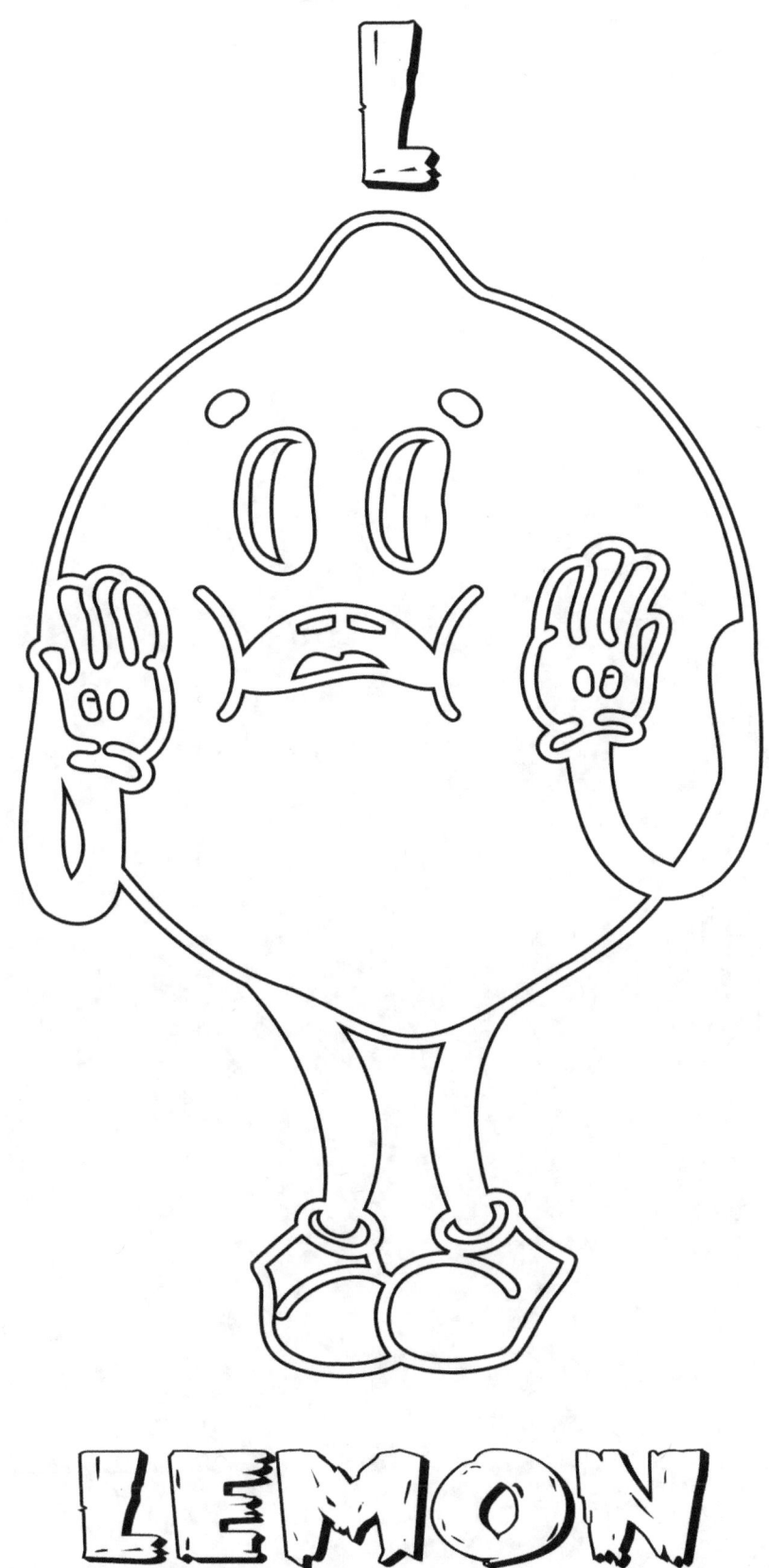

M

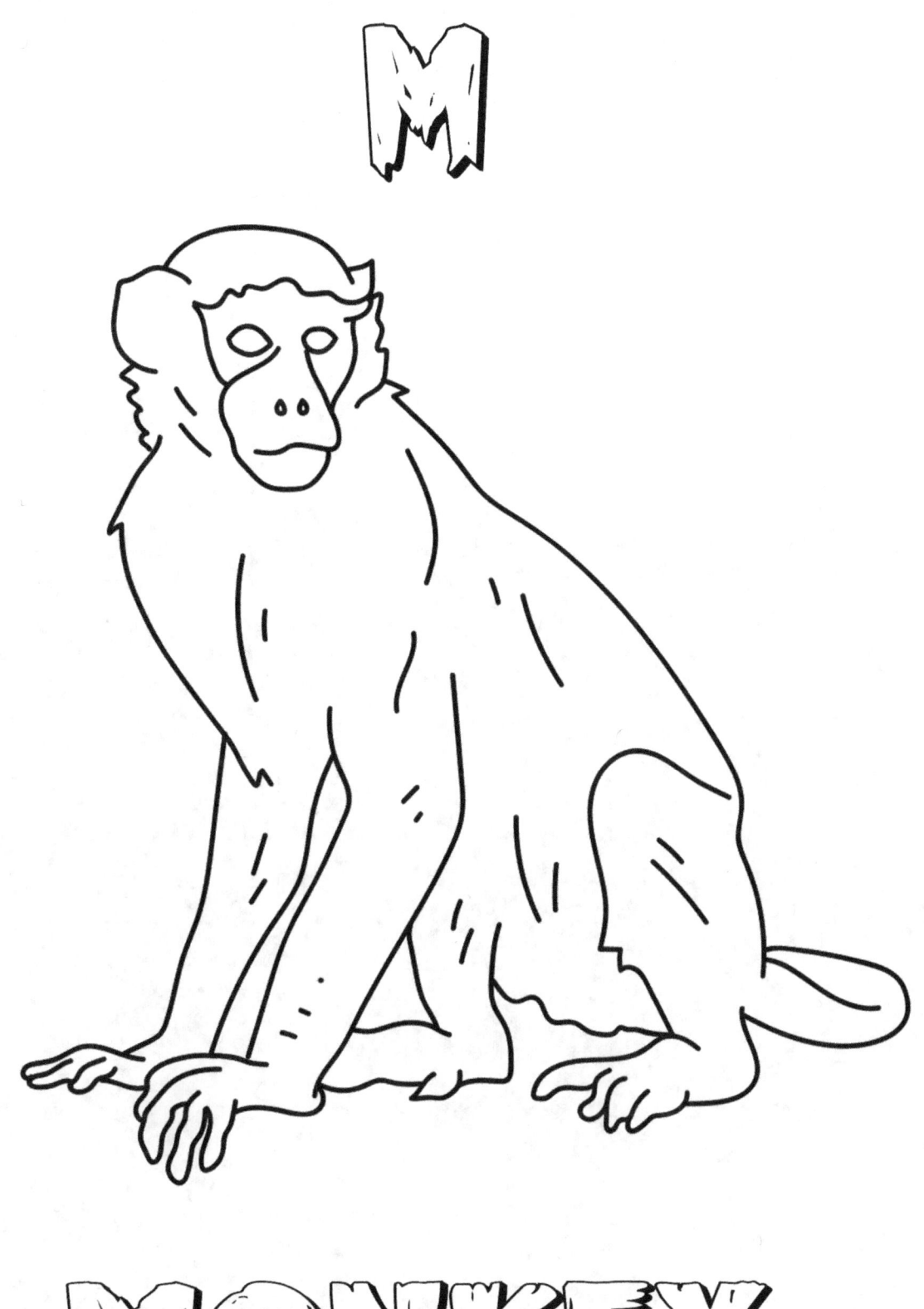

MONKEY

N

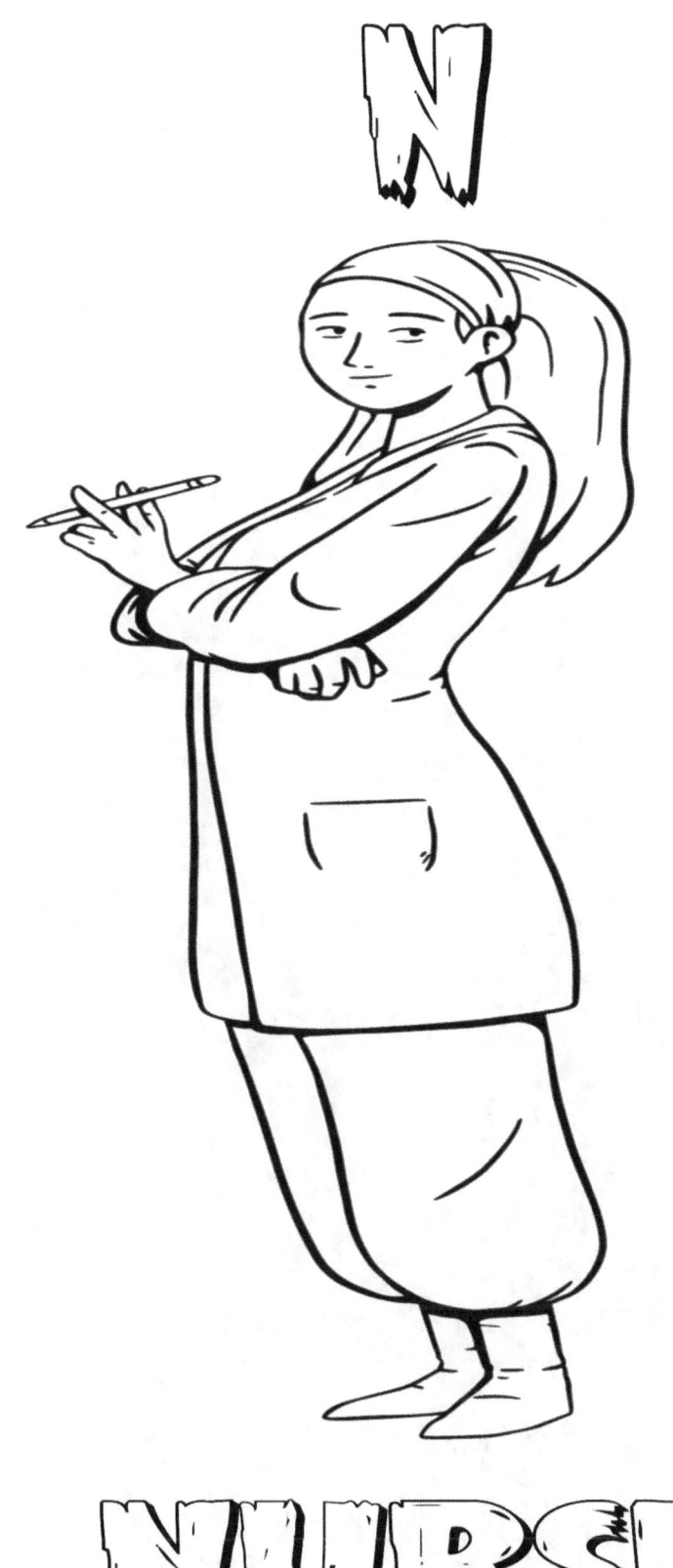

NURSE

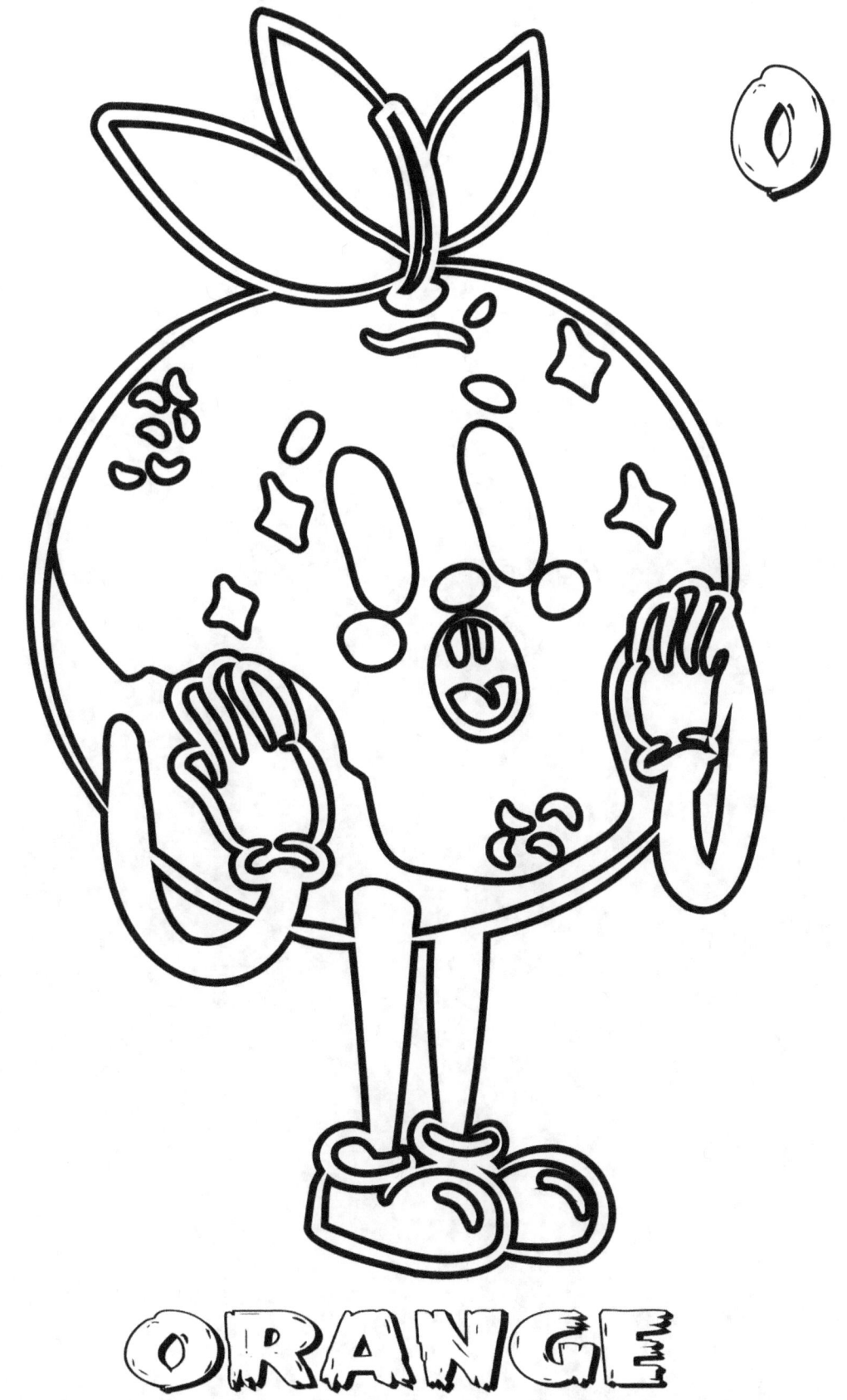

ORANGE

P

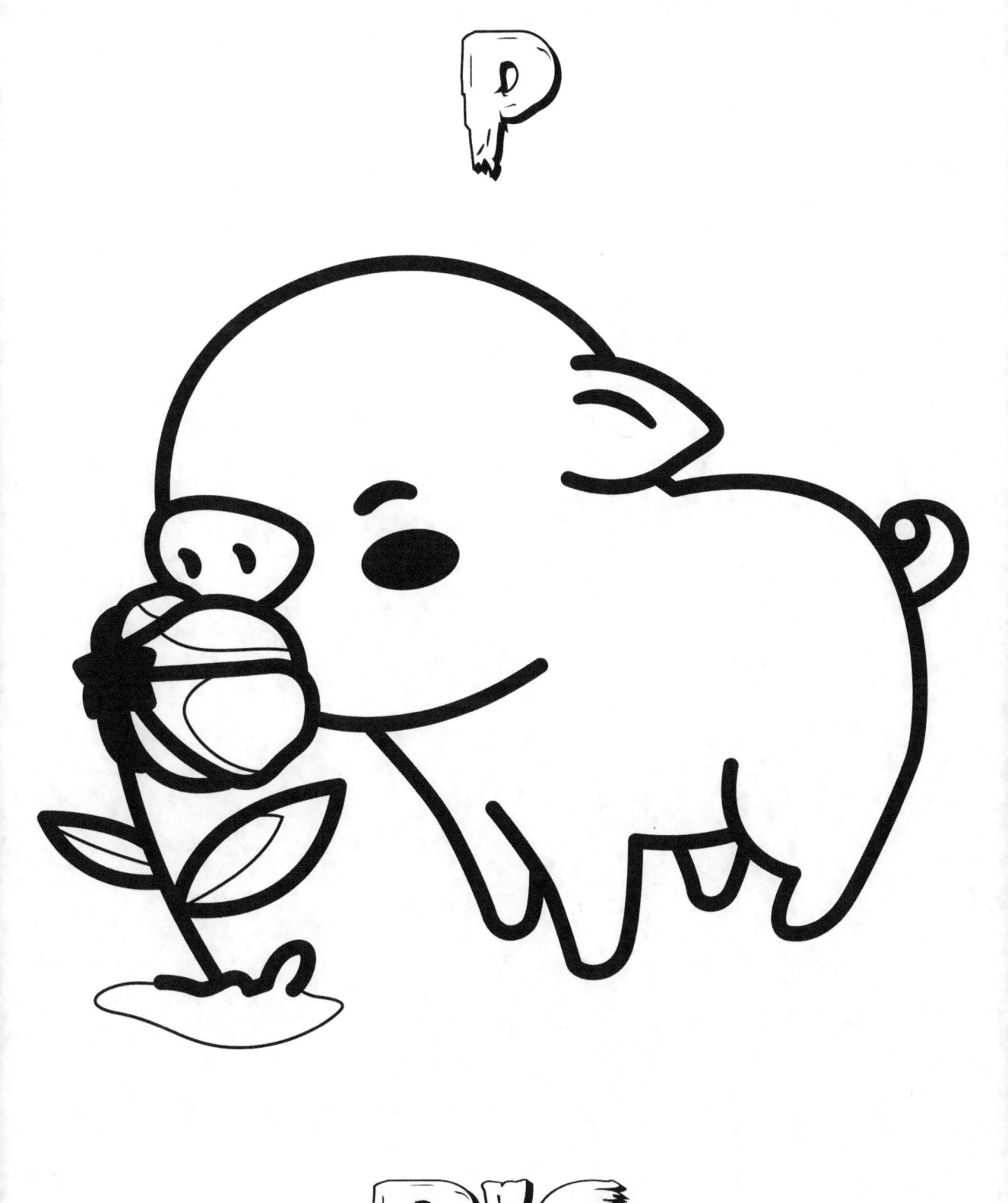

PIG

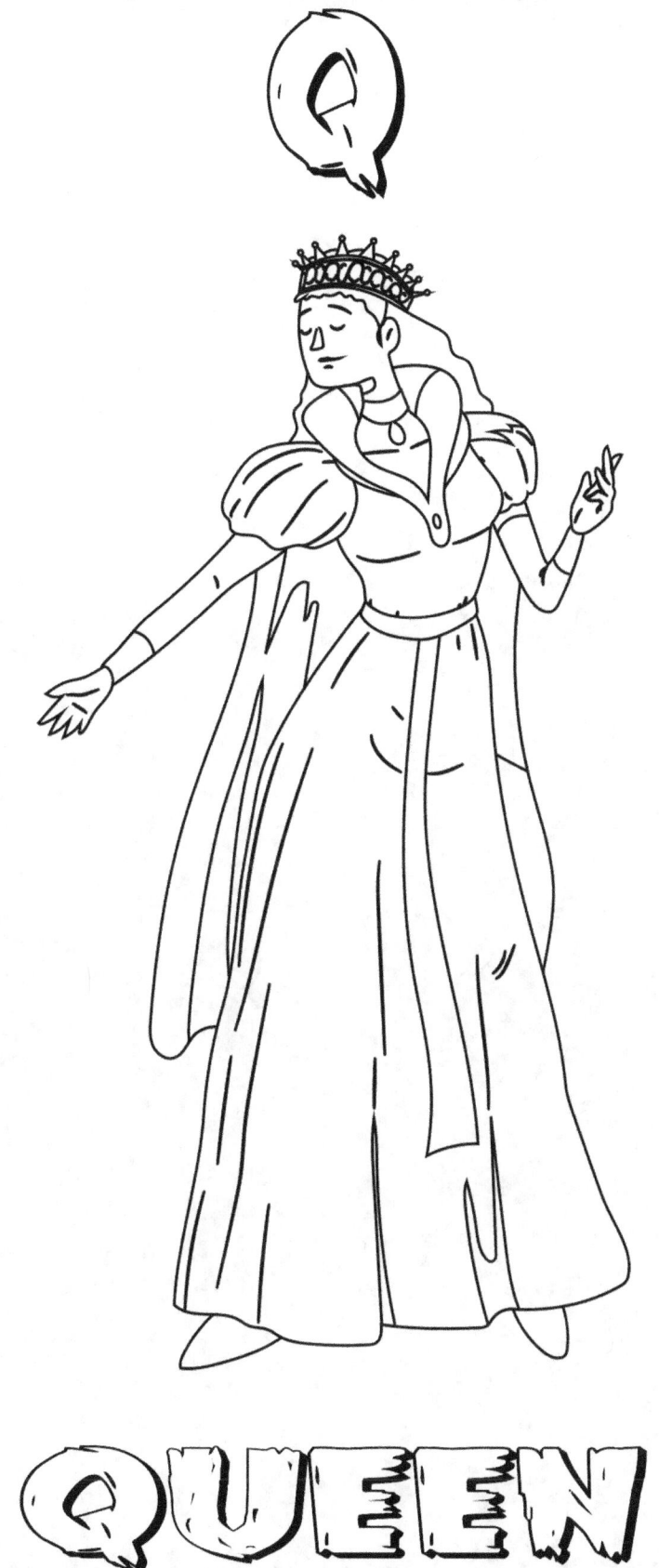

QUEEN

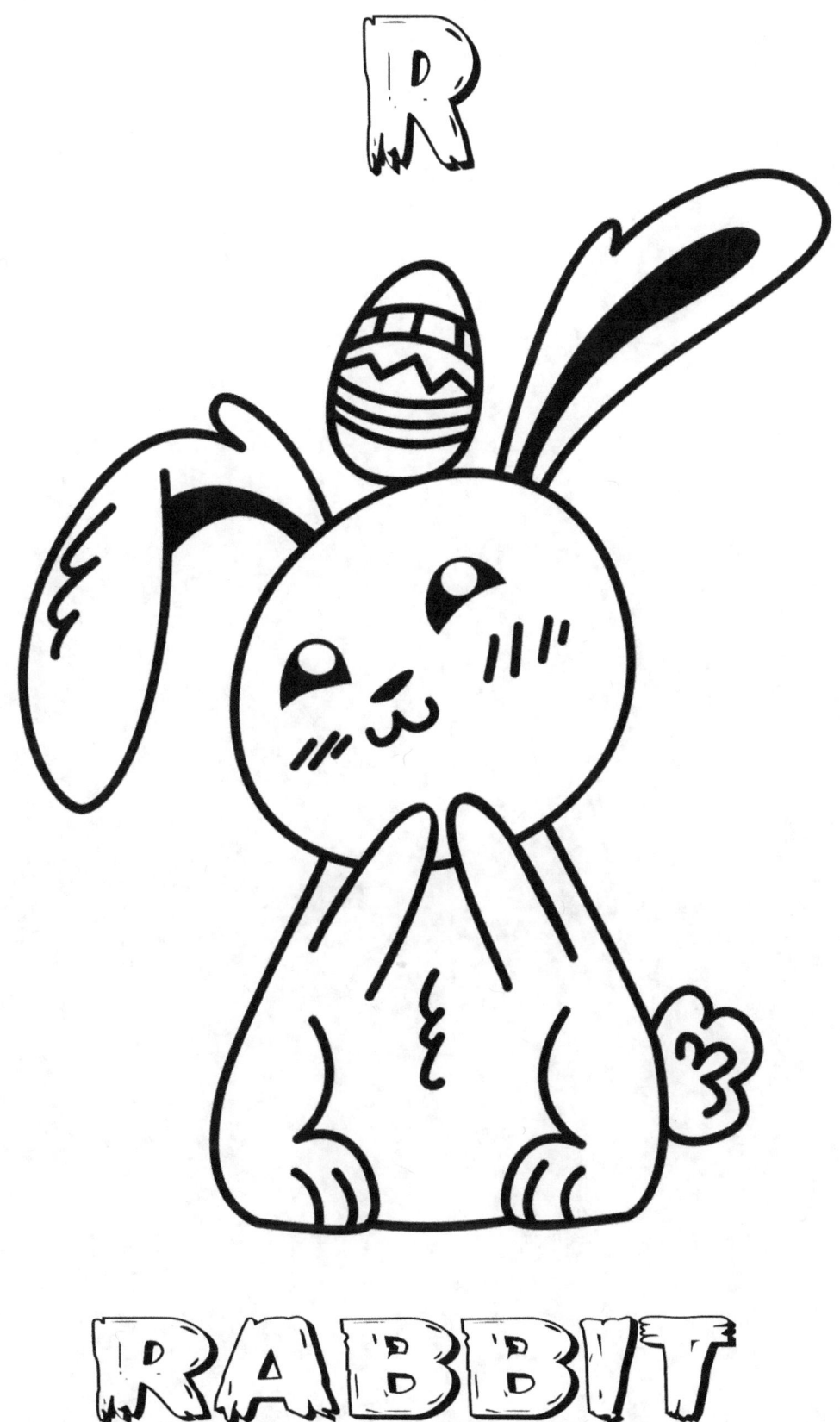

R

RABBIT

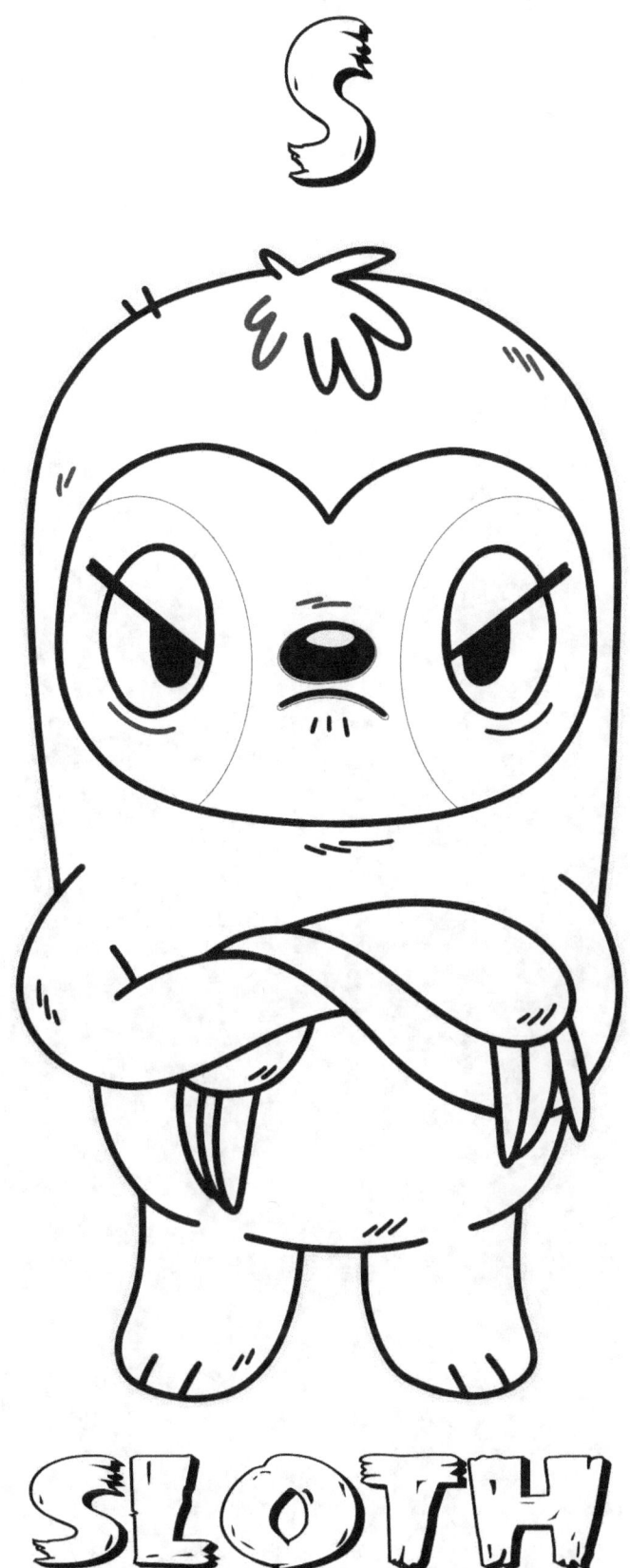

SLOTH

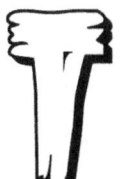

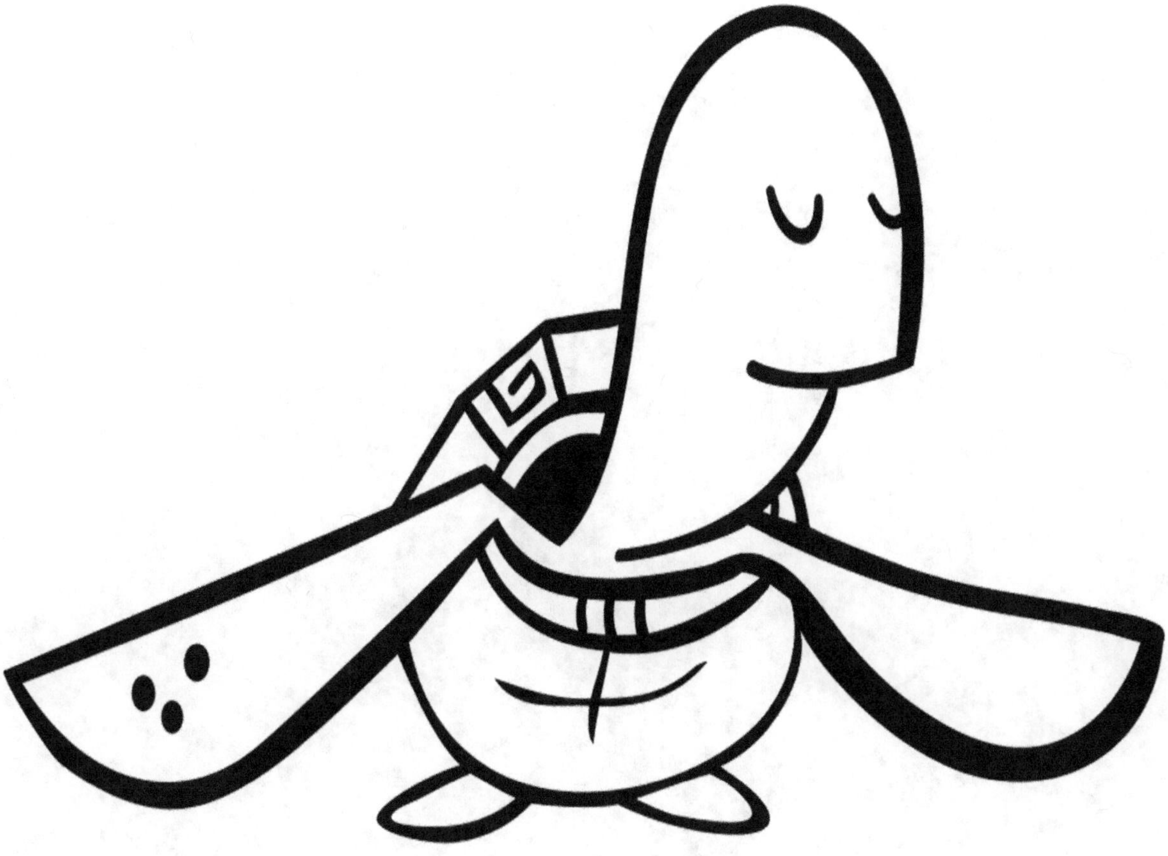

TURTLE

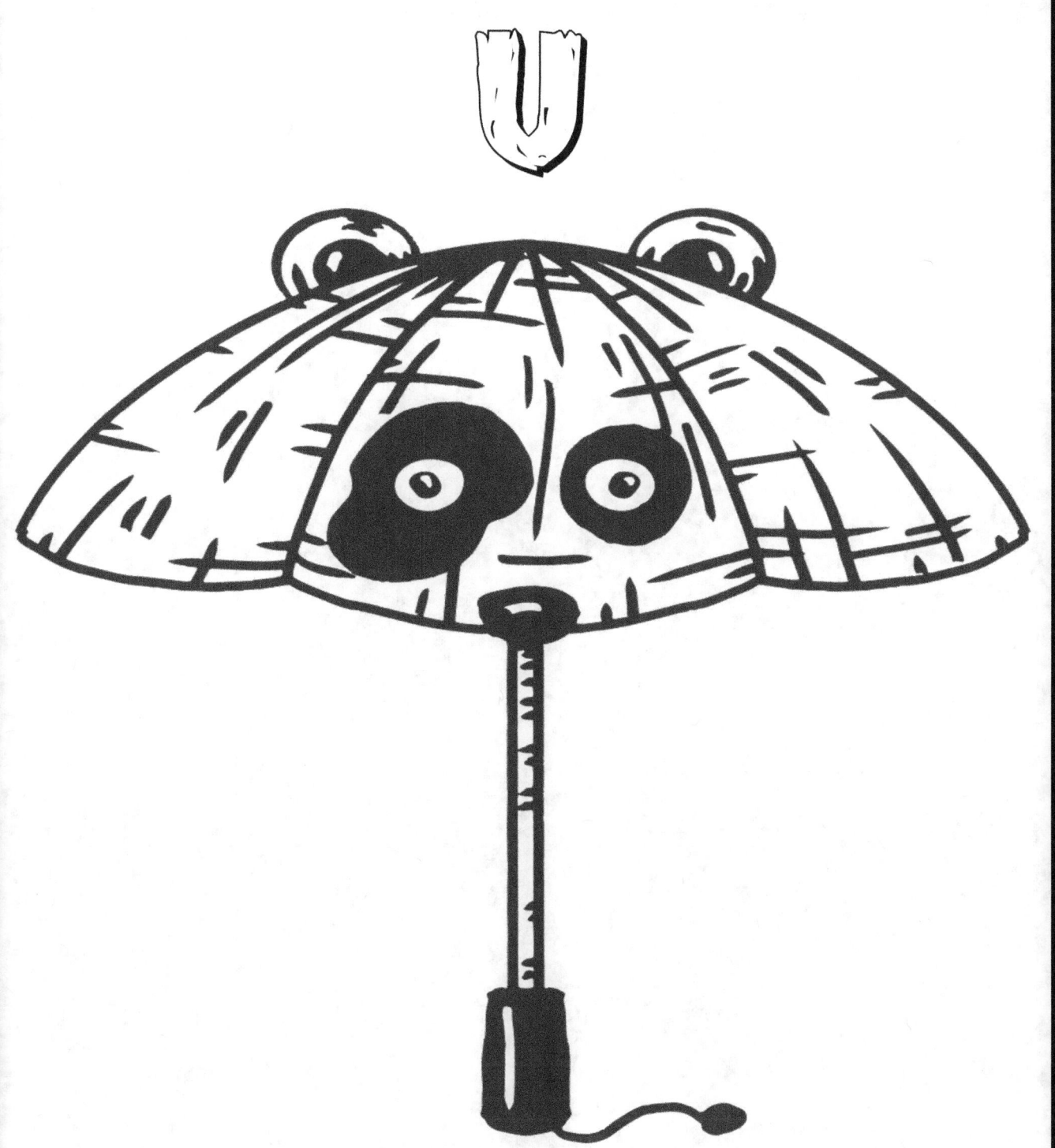

UMBRELLA

V

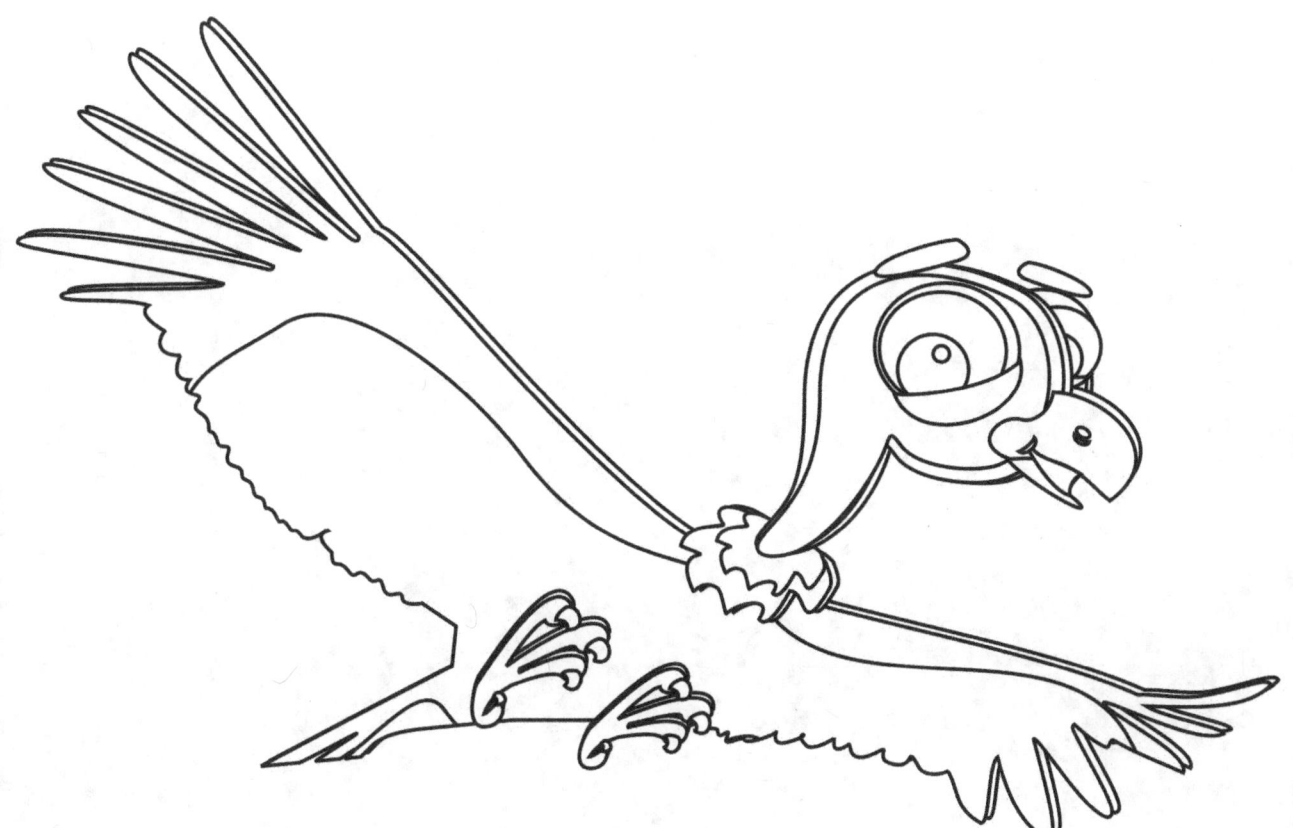

VULTURE

W

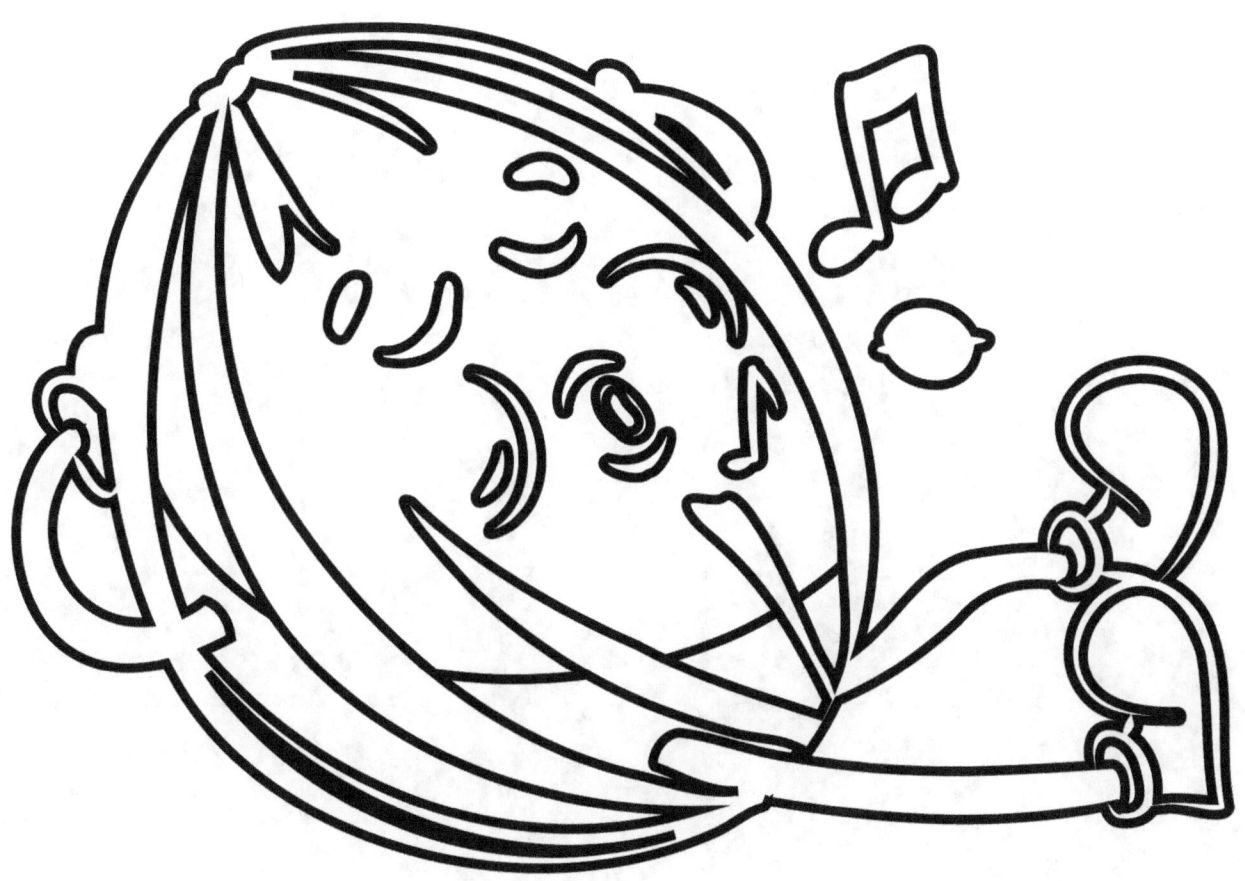

WATERMELON

X

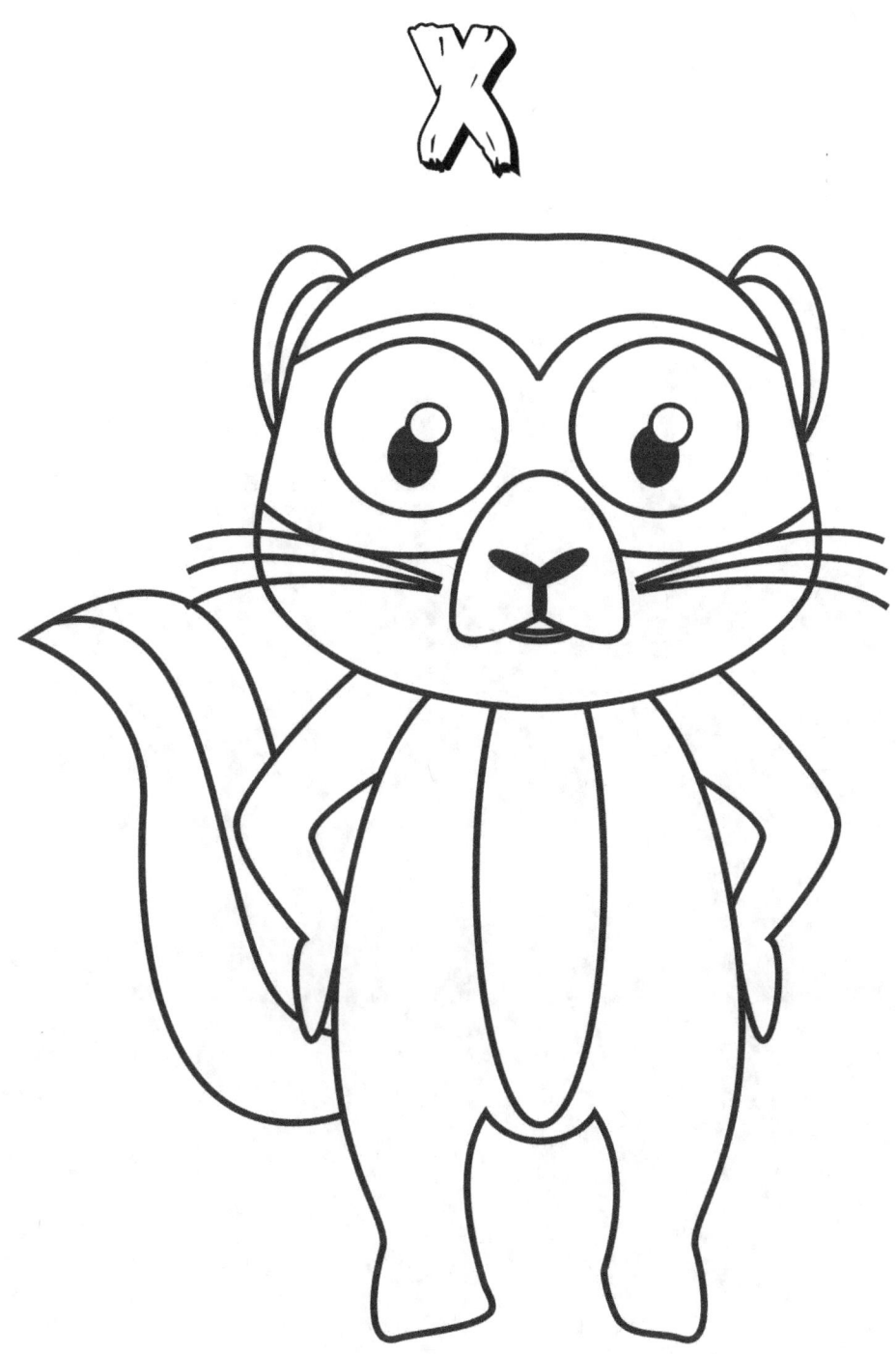

XERUS

Y

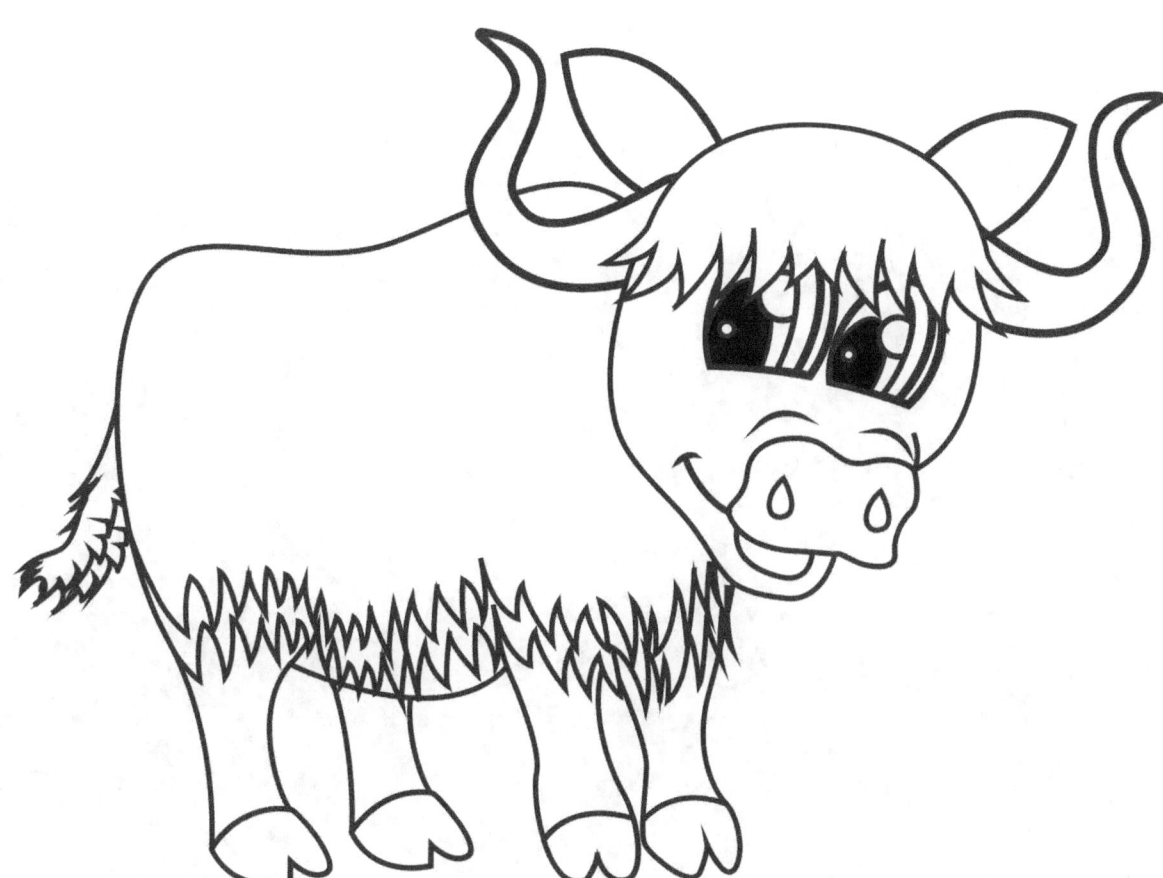

YAK

Z

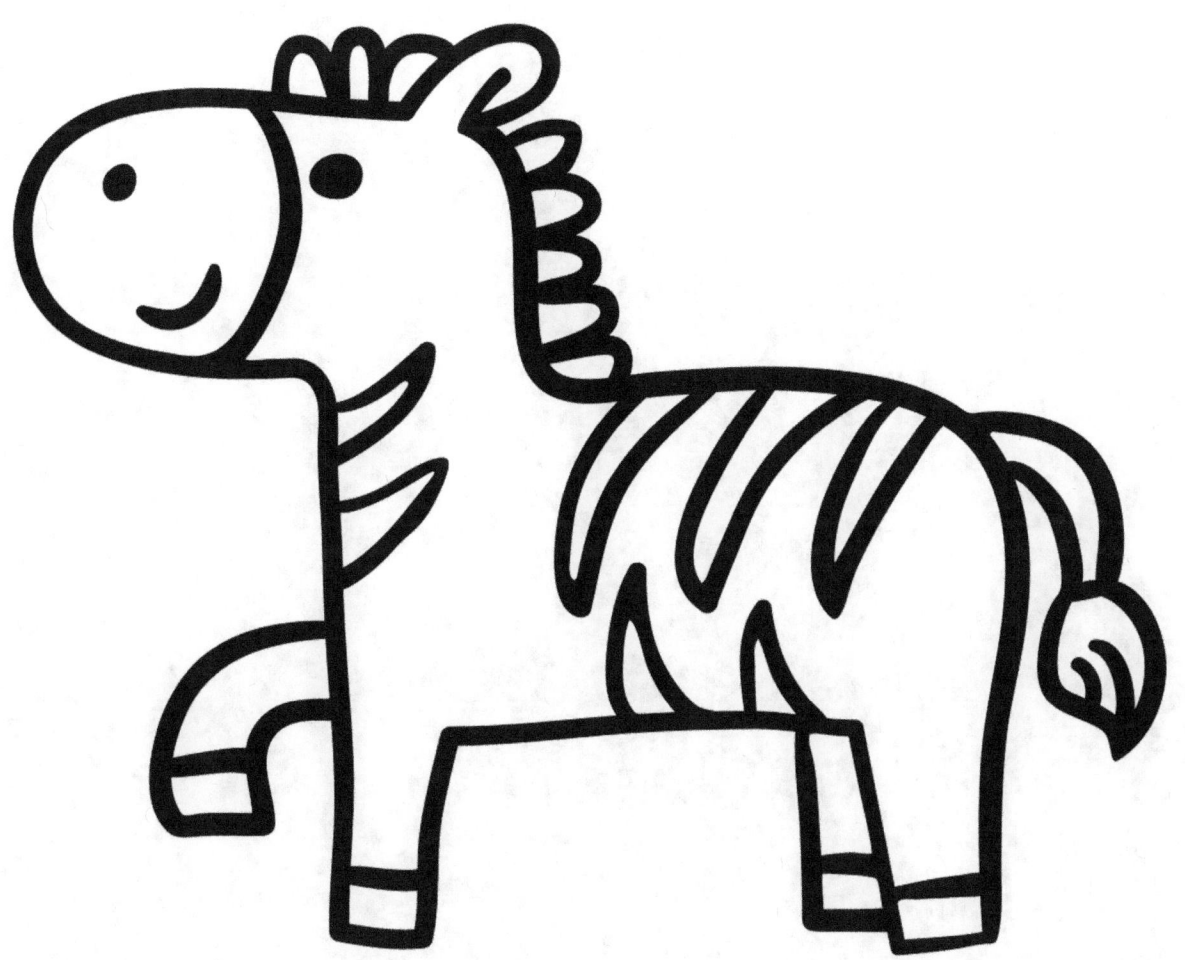

ZEBRA

www.ingramcontent.com/pod-product-compliance
Lightning Source LLC
Chambersburg PA
CBHW081004220526
45467CB00008B/2697